Rescuing the Children

RESCUING
THE
CHILDREN
The Story of the Kindertransport

DEBORAH HODGE

TUNDRA BOOKS

For the Kinder and their families,
in remembrance of the past and with hope for the future.

_____

Published in Canada by Tundra Books, a division of Random House of Canada Limited,
One Toronto Street, Suite 300, Toronto, Ontario M5C 2V6

Published in the United States by Tundra Books of Northern New York,
P.O. Box 1030, Plattsburgh, New York 12901

Library of Congress Control Number: 2011938776

Library and Archives Canada Cataloguing in Publication

Hodge, Deborah
    Rescuing the children : the story of the Kindertransport / by Deborah Hodge.

Includes index.

ISBN 978-1-77049-256-1

    1. World War, 1939-1945 – Jews – Rescue-Juvenile literature. 2. Kindertransports (Rescue operations) – Juvenile literature. 3. Jewish children in the Holocaust – Juvenile literature. 4. Refugee children – Biography – Juvenile literature.
5. Jewish refugees – Biography – Juvenile literature. I. Title.

D804.6.H63 2012   j940.53'1835083   C2011-906508-8

We acknowledge the financial support of the Government of Canada through the Canada Book Fund and that of the Government of Ontario through the Ontario Media Development Corporation's Ontario Book Initiative. We further acknowledge the support of the Canada Council for the Arts and the Ontario Arts Council for our publishing program.

ONTARIO ARTS COUNCIL
CONSEIL DES ARTS DE L'ONTARIO

Printed and bound in China

1 2 3 4 5 6   17 16 15 14 13 12

CONTENTS

FOREWORD BY IRENE N. WATTS

Irene N. Watts (formerly Irene Kirstein) was seven years old when she left Berlin on the Kindertransport.

Throughout history, even in the worst of times, stories of exceptional courage have come to light. An individual or a small group of people hides someone who is in danger from the enemy. Another in need is led across a heavily guarded frontier. A piece of bread is handed to a starving child . . . .

Irene Kirstein (now Irene N. Watts) at school in Berlin a year before she left on the Kindertransport.

Deborah Hodge's book tells us about not just a few instances but of many, of ten thousand children who were saved. We read of exceptional acts of kindness, devotion, and bravery that allowed the rescue to happen. It is a story of an exodus of hope for survival, at a time when an entire people were in despair.

Why were the children at risk? What made parents send their children to strangers? What happened to the children after they fled? This is the story that Deborah Hodge felt compelled to write, and she has done so with insight, accuracy, and compassion.

Remembering those years, they seem like a tale written by the Brothers Grimm:

Once upon a time there was a country ruled by a wicked tyrant. He was filled with hatred for anything and anyone he considered to be non-Aryan.

Most of all he hated the Jews. Their right to exist was in peril. He passed laws against them that took away every right all of us today take for granted.

Even their choice of names was denied them: Jews were forced to change their names to Sara or Israel, another way the Nazis singled them out for humiliation and punishment. Jewish means of livelihood were taken away. Their children became outcasts; they were expelled from school and forbidden to take part in normal activities, such as walking in the park, playing games, and seeing a movie. Adults were imprisoned arbitrarily – their every moment was lived overshadowed by danger.

I was born two years before Hitler came to power. I did not fully understand the fear that filled the streets, the tension and whispers in my home. Why did my mother make me stay home from kindergarten, why wasn't I allowed to see the latest Shirley Temple movie, why did I have to hide my Star of David necklace when we went out?

My father was arrested and sent to Sachsenhausen concentration camp. The fathers of my Jewish friends were taken away, too. When my father was released, I was afraid. I hardly recognized him. He sat in his chair and looked so old and thin. His hair had turned white, but there was only stubble showing because his head had been shaved.

Soon after his return, my mother said I was going to England, going on a holiday, by train and boat. Because I was a big girl now, seven and a half, she would let me travel by myself. She had a blue silk ankle-length party dress made for me. Maybe I would be invited to have tea with the little English princesses at Buckingham Palace?

When we got to the station very early on the morning of December 10, 1938, I was surprised to see so many children going on holiday too. Why were the grown-ups crying? I didn't cry – I was thrilled about my holiday. As soon as the train pulled out of the station, I took off my long, scratchy stockings. Mother had made me wear three pairs of underwear because, she said, England was cold in December.

The reality of the parting did not sink in until I reached London. I looked for my mother on the platform, but she wasn't there. That moment is still fresh in my mind. She had lied because it was the only way she could bear to send me away.

You will read of many other Kinder and their experiences, but we all have something in common: we are grateful for the new lives we were given.

The memories of those so long-ago days have grown faded – put away in the small suitcases we carried. *Rescuing the Children: The Story of the Kindertransport* makes sure that for future generations they will not fade. We will not be forgotten.

Irene N. Watts

THE CHILDREN'S RESCUE

Over seventy years ago, nine months before World War II, Irene Kirstein boarded a train in Berlin, Germany, and traveled to England without her parents. She was just seven years old.

Irene was one of the nearly ten thousand Jewish children who were saved from almost certain death at the hands of the Nazis. These children were rescued by compassionate people who organized the

TOP: *Some of the ten thousand children who were saved by the Kindertransport.*
BOTTOM: *"Quilt 1, Square 15" by Ilse F. Camis (Gross), showing Ilse waving good-bye to her grandmother. This image is one of the squares in a memory quilt made by Kinder and their families to commemorate their rescue on the Kindertransport.*
OPPOSITE: *These girls look out a train window as they leave Germany for the safety of Britain.*

Kindertransport rescue mission – and by the parents who let their children go. (The word *Kindertransport* comes from *Kinder*, the German word for *children*, and *transport*, which means *to move*.)

The Jewish children left their homes and families in Germany, Austria, Czechoslovakia, and the Free City of Danzig (now Gdańsk, Poland). They journeyed across Europe to Britain on trains, boats, and planes without their parents. They traveled to a new country and a new life. Although they didn't know it at the time, many of the children would never see their parents again.

In the Talmud, the Jewish holy book, there is a saying: "Whoever saves one life saves the world entire."

Who were the Kinder and why did they need to be saved? Who helped the children? What happened after they were saved? What can we learn from this rescue mission today?

This is the story of the Kindertransport.

MEET THE CHILDREN

Each of the nearly ten thousand children who were rescued has a story. Here are eight girls and boys you can get to know. They tell their stories in their own words throughout this book.

RUTH OPPENHEIMER (now Ruth David)
Ruth was ten years old when she left Frankfurt, Germany, on the Kindertransport. She lived with her family in Fränkisch-Crumbach, in the countryside. She had two sisters and three brothers.

ELLEN AUSTER (now Ellen Fletcher)
Ellen lived in a group home with other children in Berlin, Germany. Her mother lived nearby but was a working mom and could not care for her. Ellen was ten years old when she traveled on the Kindertransport.

JOSEPH HABERER
Joseph left on the Kindertransport when he was nine years old. He lived with his parents and foster brother in Villingen, Germany.

HEDY WACHENHEIMER (now Hedy Epstein)
Hedy lived with her parents in Kippenheim, Germany. She was fourteen years old when she left on the Kindertransport.

MIRIAM WIECK (now Miriam Schneider)

Miriam lived with her parents and brother in Königsberg, Germany. She traveled from Berlin on one of the last Kindertransports. She was thirteen years old. This is a photo of her as a baby.

HANS LEVY

Hans lived with his parents, sister, and brother in Gladbeck, Germany. He was eleven years old when he and his brother went to Holland on the Kindertransport. When Hans was thirteen, he and his brother escaped to England on a ship called the SS *Bodegraven*. He is a young man in this photo.

NORBERT RIPP

Norbert lived with his parents and brothers in Wanne-Eickel, Germany. When he was eleven years old, his mother took him to the last railroad station before the Dutch border and put him on a train to Holland. Later, he fled to England on the SS *Bodegraven*.

DORA GOSTYNSKI (now Doris Small)

After Dora's parents died, she and her sister were turned out of their home by the landlord. Family friends took them in. Dora was fourteen years old when she left Berlin on the Kindertransport.

TERROR IN GERMANY

For Jews in the 1930s, Germany was a terrifying place.

Adolf Hitler, leader of the Nazi party, came to power in 1933 and carried out a long and cruel hate campaign against Jews, one that had begun when he became leader of the party in 1921. Fierce anti-Semitism, or discrimination against Jews, spread throughout the country.

Although it wasn't true, Hitler and many German citizens believed that Jewish people were responsible for the shortages of money, food, and jobs in Germany at the time. (In truth, many of these economic problems came about after Germany lost World War I and was forced to pay huge fines for its part in starting the first war.)

Hitler told the German people that their problems would go away if the country was "free of Jews." He told them not to have Jewish friends; not to shop at Jewish stores; and not to use the services of Jewish doctors, lawyers, and other professional people. Books by Jewish authors were burned.

There were signs everywhere banning Jews from movie theaters, restaurants, parks, skating rinks, swimming pools, and other public places. The signs said such things as "Dogs and Jews not admitted" and "The Jews are our misfortune." Radio broadcasts and newspapers were full of anti-Jewish hate messages.

At school, non-Jewish children were taught to love Hitler and to hate Jews. And all non-Jewish children aged ten to seventeen were made to join Nazi youth groups, such as the Hitler Youth, where their beliefs were shaped by Nazi teachings.

In 1935, things got worse. Hitler's government passed the Nuremberg Laws, which took away the right of Jews to be citizens. By 1938, Jewish children could no longer go to public school.

OPPOSITE: *"Burning of the Books" by Hans Jackson. The Nazis burned books written by Jewish authors.*
TOP: *"Boycott" by Hans Jackson, showing the boycott (or shunning) of the Berlin store belonging to his parents.*
BOTTOM: *"Leaving Germany for Kitchener Camp" by Hans Jackson, depicting Nazi soldiers harassing Hans as he flees Germany.*

HANS JACKSON

Hans was a Jewish teenager living in Berlin in the 1930s. He escaped to England in 1939 when he was eighteen years old. He was able to flee Nazi Germany because he was a trained carpenter and had a job waiting for him in England. Later, when he was an adult, he created many powerful paintings and drawings of his time in Germany. Much of the art in this book is by Hans.

VOICES OF THE CHILDREN

Although many of the Kinder are in their eighties today, they still have vivid memories of what it was like being young and Jewish in Nazi Germany. Here are some of their stories.

RUTH'S STORY

Ruth remembers the day she was told she couldn't go to public school anymore.

> "We were outcasts. I no longer wanted to be out-of-doors – life seemed too unsafe. Notices had gone up outside swimming pools, cinemas, skating rinks, and other places of recreation, denying entry to Jews. My dream of swimming lessons was now impossible."

ELLEN'S STORY

Ellen celebrated her tenth birthday just before she left on the Kindertransport.

"My mother planned a big party both to celebrate my birthday and as a farewell party. We were in the kitchen the day before the party, and the radio was on. Suddenly, we heard an announcement. No Jews would be allowed on the streets the following day. The only person who could come to my 'party' was a friend of my mother's – Tante [Aunt] Dora, as she was known to me. She was a non-Jew married to a Jewish man who had been taken away by the Nazis earlier that year."

OPPOSITE: *"School Expulsion" by Hans Jackson. A Jewish child is expelled from school.*
RIGHT: *"Harassing the Children" by Hans Jackson, showing Jewish children being bullied by Hitler Youth.*

JOSEPH'S STORY

Joseph was one of two Jewish children at his school. He remembers the other children, who belonged to the Hitler Youth.

"They would throw stones, use slingshots, call me names, and harass me when I walked back and forth to school. There was a sign at the park that said '*Juden Verboten*' (Jews forbidden). You couldn't go to the swimming pool. You couldn't do this and you couldn't do that – all of this raised the question: Why me?"

DESPERATE TIMES

Under Hitler's rule, Jewish workers lost their jobs. Jewish families were forced to give up their businesses, properties, and possessions. Men were beaten in the streets or arrested and sent to concentration (prison) camps. Money was scarce. People were frightened. The risk of violence was everywhere.

In March 1938, Hitler's armies took control of Austria and, later, the part of Czechoslovakia called the Sudetenland. Jews in these countries were in great danger, too.

Fearing for their lives, great numbers of Jews tried to escape to other countries. They were allowed to leave but were forced to abandon most of their money and belongings.

In July 1938, President Franklin D. Roosevelt of the United States organized a conference of representatives from thirty-two countries to discuss the problems of Austrian and German Jews. The Evian Conference, held over eight days in France, did little to help. When it ended, most countries had found reasons not to take in the Jewish refugees. (Refugees are people fleeing danger in their own country and looking for safety in another country.)

Why did they turn away people who needed help? The Great Depression caused hard times in many countries, and these countries didn't want to share what little money and few jobs they did have with

LEFT: *Jewish girls who escaped Nazi Germany arrive at British customs in 1938.*
OPPOSITE: *Ellen Auster's mother's passport which shows the name Sara and the letter J.*

impoverished refugees, who would need their help and care. Also, anti-Semitism was common in many countries in those days. In Canada in the 1930s, for example, Jews were barred from many jobs and public places, like golf courses and hotels.

Visas (permission documents to enter a new country) now became very difficult to get. The world had turned its back on the refugees.

The Nazis forced Jews to adopt the names Sara (for girls and women) and Israel (for boys and men). Jewish passports also had a big red J (for *Jew*) stamped on them. These identifying labels made it even harder for the refugees to leave.

By 1939, about three hundred thousand Jews – roughly 60 percent of the German Jewish population from 1933 – had managed to leave Germany. Many more Jews would have escaped Nazi Europe if other countries had been willing to accept them as new citizens to their country.

THE NIGHT OF BROKEN GLASS

On November 9 and 10, 1938, in cities and towns throughout Germany, Austria, and the Sudetenland, Jews were targeted in a wave of violent Nazi-led attacks. During the night, mobs of SA men (members of the Nazi paramilitary) and Hitler Youth went on an anti-Jewish rampage. They broke into thousands of Jewish businesses, schools, community centers, hospitals, cemeteries, and homes. They smashed windows, stole possessions, and terrorized people.

The mobs also burned down hundreds of synagogues (Jewish places of worship) as police and firefighters stood by to prevent non-Jewish properties from burning.

Nearly one hundred Jews were killed, and up to thirty thousand Jewish men were arrested and sent to concentration camps.

There was so much broken glass in the streets that this night of Nazi violence became known as *Kristallnacht*, which means "Crystal Night" – more commonly called the Night of Broken Glass.

It was clear that under Nazi rule, no Jewish person was safe. People were desperate to escape.

RUTH'S STORY

"I awoke to thunderous knocking on the door. Apparently, it was not opened quickly enough, as I could hear the blows of an ax and wood crashing, then shouting and screaming. My Aunt Ida was beaten by the thugs. My sister Hannah came into my room. We were terrified. The house had a back staircase that led down to an inner courtyard. Hannah and I fled downstairs, away from the tumult, barefoot in our nightdresses. It was a cold, winter night. Father's car stood there. What else could we do? We jumped in and cowered together in the back. I cannot say how long we remained in our hiding place; it seemed like many hours of shivering with cold and panic. I know that what I experienced there, at the age of nine, was the greatest fear I have ever known."

ELLEN'S STORY

"We children had gone to sleep. The housemother woke us up and told us all to get dressed, even with coats, hats, and gloves. We were to sit silently on our beds, in the dark. She was sobbing. We could hear much noise outside – shouting, screaming, bashing, and running – and the windows were lit with one or more fires. Our housemother fully expected the Nazis to crash into the apartment."

LEFT: *"Burning Synagogue Kristallnacht" by Hans Jackson, showing one of the hundreds of synagogues set on fire by the Nazis that night.*
TOP: *"Parent's Home and Shop Kristallnacht" by Hans Jackson, depicting the smashing of windows of the store belonging to his parents.*

SAVING THE CHILDREN

Even though people around the world were shocked by the events of *Kristallnacht*, very few countries were willing to relax their immigration laws and accept the Jewish refugees. Britain was different.

Immediately following *Kristallnacht*, a British delegation including Jewish leaders and members of the Religious Society of Friends (or Quakers) made an urgent plea to their government to allow Jewish children to come to safety in Britain. (Quakers are a faith group whose members believe in working for peace and justice, and making the world a better place.) The government agreed to help.

Children under the age of seventeen were allowed to enter Britain under certain conditions. The costs for their education and care –

including a fifty pound sterling deposit for the eventual return to their home country – were to be paid by private citizens or organizations. Also, the children were to come alone, without their parents. (Everyone believed the children would be gone for a short time and that they would rejoin their parents once the trouble in Germany and Austria had passed.) To speed up the rescue, the children could come without the usual travel visas. This kind act on the part of the British government meant that no time would be wasted trying to get paperwork done.

An organization known as the Movement for the Care of Children from Germany (later known as Refugee Children's Movement, or RCM) was formed of Jewish, Quaker, and

LEFT: *Two young travelers from Vienna wearing numbered identification tags.*
OPPOSITE: *Children on the first Kindertransport arrive in Harwich, England.*

Christian groups. They worked together to bring the children to Britain by raising funds, collecting clothing and equipment, arranging travel plans, finding sponsors, and organizing placements from the many offers of accommodation they received. The organization also sent representatives to Germany and Austria to set up the travel arrangements from there.

The Nazis agreed to let the children leave as long as they did not take anything of value with them.

Jewish parents understood that their families were in grave danger. When they heard about the rescue mission, they rushed to register their children for it.

The first Kindertransport left the Berlin train station on December 1, 1938. On board were almost two hundred Jewish children whose orphanage had been burned down on *Kristallnacht*.

THE KINDERTRANSPORT

No parent wants to send their child away, but the Jewish parents knew that their children were in danger. Even though they could not leave Nazi-ruled countries themselves, the parents did what they could to get their children out.

Many of the Kinder believe that their parents gave them life twice: once when they were born and a second time when they were sent to safety on the Kindertransport.

NORBERT'S STORY

"My parents faced a terrible dilemma, a dilemma no parent of small children should ever have to face. Convinced that we could not leave Germany in the foreseeable future, they decided to send me, at age eleven, to the safety of Holland – where I would be at the mercy of strangers in a strange land, without knowing the language or when we would see each other again."

HEDY'S STORY

"In 1939, thanks to my parents' great love for me, I was able to leave Germany on a Kindertransport to England. My parents gave me a second life."

In Germany, the offices of refugee organizations were flooded with urgent requests from parents and relatives to send their children to Britain.

About a thousand children a month were able to leave. They ranged from three months to sixteen years of age. The children who were chosen to go were most often the ones at greatest risk, including those who had been orphaned, had parents in a concentration camp, or were homeless. Other children were just lucky to get a spot.

The children were sent in groups of several hundred at a time. Most of them boarded special trains in large cities such as Berlin, Frankfurt, Vienna, and Prague. Those who lived in smaller places traveled to the big cities to join the transports.

The trains passed through Germany and crossed the border into Holland or Belgium. From a port city, such as the Hook of Holland, the children boarded a ship to Harwich, England. From there, many of them rode another train to London, where they were met by sponsors – organizations or people who had agreed to pay the costs and be responsible for the children. (Children without sponsors were sent to hostels and holiday camps instead.)

Not all the Kinder traveled by train. An early group left by ship from the port of Hamburg, Germany. Other children flew by plane from Czechoslovakia. The last group left Holland by ship in 1940 – just as the country fell to German forces.

The first transport left Berlin on December 1, 1938, and the last transport left from Germany on September 1, 1939 – the day Germany invaded Poland and war was declared. After that, the borders were closed and travel was halted.

TOP: *Young refugees from Germany and Austria on the train.*
BOTTOM: *"Quilt 1, Square 8" by Margaret and Kenneth Lowe, showing Gretel Pappenheimer's journey from Munich to London. Gretel is now called Margaret Lowe.*

GETTING READY

Once children were accepted for the transport, parents hurried to get them ready.

The Kinder were only allowed to take what they could carry and nothing of value. They were permitted to take a small amount of money (only ten reichsmarks, worth about four dollars).

Anxious parents had to decide what to pack. What could they fit into one little suitcase?

They packed clothes for England as well as family photographs and mementos, a toy or doll, and prayer books or other religious items – special things to remind the children of home. Some children took a musical instrument, such as a violin or recorder, that they could carry in their arms.

In the days and hours before the children departed, parents gave last-minute blessings and advice for the journey and life in England.

Although they desperately hoped to be reunited, family members did not know when they would see each other again. Many parents told their children that they would follow them to Britain as soon as they could.

MIRIAM'S STORY

"My father gave me one of his violins to take – one of his most valuable ones. I still have it. Music helped me when there was no one else. It made things more bearable and gave me a place to go."

IRENE'S STORY

"When I was a small girl living in Berlin, my grandfather gave me a puppet theater. A year later, my family sent me on the Kindertransport. I left both family and theater behind. At age seven, I discovered that stories can travel with you wherever you go."

OPPOSITE: Many of the children carried a favorite toy or doll as comfort.

TOP: Irene's mother reads a story to Irene and her brother.

LEFT: "Quilt 1, Square 6" by Ruth Adler, who remembers leaving Prague with her belongings and an identification tag around her neck.

RUTH'S STORY

"The night before my departure, both my parents gave me a blessing. That is, they laid their hands on me and said a prayer commending me to God's care:

The Lord bless you and keep you;
The Lord look kindly upon you and be gracious unto you;
The Lord bestow favor upon you and give you peace.

There was little else my mother and father could do. I can imagine their thoughts and emotions."

TOP: *The label from Margot Stern's suitcase.*
LEFT: *Heinz Stephan Lewy with his father and stepmother before he left on a Kindertransport to France.*

SAYING GOOD-BYE

Saying good-bye was a heartbreaking experience for the families. Parents hugged and kissed their children. They asked them to write letters and stay in touch. Everyone, including the children, tried to be brave, for no one knew what the future would hold.

Many of the trains left the station at night and parents were not allowed onto the platform. They had to say their good-byes inside the waiting rooms. (The Nazis did not want a public scene that would draw attention to the plight of these refugee children.)

It took tremendous courage for these parents to send their children on the transport. But they did it – and they gave their children the gift of freedom and life.

"Children Leaving Anhalter Bahnhof" by Hans Jackson. Kinder say good-bye to their parents at the Berlin train station.

ELLEN'S STORY

"I left Berlin on December 14, 1938. My mother and new stepfather took me to the railway station in a taxi early in the morning. The scene in the station's waiting room was a very emotional one. The parents were saying good-bye to their children, some as young as toddlers, not knowing what would happen to them – or to themselves."

HANS LEVY'S STORY

"When we arrived at the station, there was already a long queue of children and parents at the barrier. When the official arrived to open the barrier, he shouted, 'Children only, children only!' The parents protested, not being able to take their children to their seats on the train. In the confusion, I heard the voice of my father shouting, 'Come back! You haven't said good-bye to your mother!' But being driven forward and carrying heavy suitcases, it was not possible to turn back."

OPPOSITE: *Children and parents say a final farewell at Schlesischer Bahnhof, Berlin, November 1938.*
RIGHT: *"Quilt 2, Square 16" by Helga Newman, who was nine years old when she said good-bye to her parents in Vienna, Austria.*

NORBERT'S STORY

"On January 20, 1939, my mother took me by train to Aachen, the last major railroad station before the Dutch border, and put me on a local train for Holland. The last view I had of my mother was of her standing all alone on the platform, with tears streaming down her cheeks, as the train slowly pulled out of the station."

HEDY'S STORY

"There were five hundred children on my train. The oldest was seventeen; the youngest were six-month-old twins. Before we left, I remember a lot of arms and hands in the window. I heard someone say, 'Please take good care of our babies.' I remember my parents running along the platform, getting smaller and smaller, and then they were gone."

THE JOURNEY

The children's journey by train and boat took several days. The main route was across Germany to the Dutch border, then through Holland to the port city, Hook of Holland. From there, the children boarded a ship to England.

On the train, the children passed the time sleeping, eating food their parents had packed, looking out the windows, and talking to one another. Some children found the journey very long – as long as a lifetime. Some cried and were terribly upset. Many of the older children understood the seriousness of the situation. Some of the younger ones (whose parents didn't want them to worry) believed they were going on a holiday.

The older children cared for the younger ones. Babies were held and soothed by teenagers. Some of the teens played musical instruments to distract the younger children.

A few adults also helped supervise the travelers. These chaperones were Quakers or courageous young Jewish men and women who rode to Holland with the children then returned to Germany or Austria to face an uncertain future. (The Nazis threatened to end the transports if the chaperones did not return.)

While some of the Kinder felt like they were on an adventure, many remember feeling very sad at leaving their families and being worried about what the future would hold – both for themselves and for the loved ones they had left behind.

TOP: *A boy plays his violin for the other children in his compartment.*
MIDDLE: *Some children passed the time by reading.*
BOTTOM: *Jewish children are greeted by kind Dutch women in Rotterdam.*

MIRIAM'S STORY

Miriam remembers crying on the train on the way to meet her transport in Berlin and a man asking her why she was sad. She recalls her feelings.

"I just knew I was never coming back."

ELLEN'S STORY

"I was the oldest in my train compartment and took a mothering role in comforting the others who were, of course, very upset at leaving home and family. After awhile, I took out a recorder I had been permitted to take with me, and I played songs for the others to sing. It helped."

As the trains approached Holland, German border guards moved through the compartments, inspecting luggage. The children had to open their suitcases and watch in terrified silence as Nazis rummaged through their belongings in search of any valuables that they could confiscate.

Many children feared that they would not be allowed to enter Holland and would be forced to return to Germany.

ELLEN'S STORY

"As we neared the Dutch border, a uniformed customs official came into our compartment and ordered us to open our suitcases. He then wildly threw the contents around, upsetting the children all over again. After we had collectively repacked the suitcases, I again played songs on my recorder to calm everyone's nerves."

NORBERT'S STORY

When Norbert reached the Dutch border, he was asked to show his travel documents.

"The passport control was conducted by a young SS (Nazi) officer. His face turned beet red when I showed him my children's passport with the big red *J*, for *Jew*, stamped on it, but I did not have the needed permission to enter Holland. He screamed at me – to the point where even the woman who shared the compartment with me turned as white as a sheet. Then he slammed the compartment door and let me go on my way. Minutes later, I was in Holland."

Once the children crossed into Holland, they felt a huge sense of relief. They cheered, shouted, and sang. They were safe!

Many of the Kinder remember the kindness of Dutch citizens who met them at the train stations and gave them delicious food and drinks – chocolate, apples, cookies, juice, and even hot meals. Some of the children recall being hugged by friendly Dutch women. Others describe the gifts of dolls or games they received.

The warm welcome from the Dutch people helped the children understand that they were safely out of Germany. This kindness made a lasting impression on the Kinder, and many of them still remember the moment.

DORA'S STORY

"When we crossed the border into Holland, I took a deep breath and thought, *I'm out of Germany.* There were Dutch women with baskets of food. They knew the children were coming, and they met us at the trains. It was unbelievable!"

ARRIVING IN ENGLAND

While some of the children stayed in Holland (either with relatives or in refugee centers), most continued their train trip across the country to the coast, where they boarded a ship to England.

It was the first time many of the Kinder had seen the ocean, and some recall how beautiful it looked. After a rough overnight crossing, with many of the children becoming seasick, the ferry docked in Harwich, England.

Children who had relatives or foster families waiting for them got on another train to London's Liverpool Street station. (Children without sponsors went to holiday camps until more permanent housing could be found.)

Volunteers greeted the trains as they arrived at the station and guided the Kinder to a reception center run by the Refugee Children's Movement. This is where the children first met their sponsors.

Imagine how the Kinder might have felt – relieved at being safe, exhausted from the long journey, nervous about meeting their foster families, confused by the new language, and sad for the loved ones they had left behind.

The Kinder were looked after by individual families or by caretakers in group homes. Some of the children went to hostels, orphanages, or boarding schools. Some lived in the city, others on farms in the countryside.

Many of the sponsors and foster families were people who had responded to the government's plea on BBC radio asking for the public's help in sheltering the children. These volunteers lived in England, Scotland, Wales, and Northern Ireland.

Transports of Jewish children arrived in England twice a week for the first few months. But by the summer of 1939, as the situation became more urgent, transports of children started arriving every day.

The citizens of Great Britain took the children in when no one else would. Without the help of these people, the Kindertransport would not have been possible.

"Quilt 1, Square 3" by Berta S. Wesler (with Karen Wesler), who remembers being given candy by a kind British man.

MIRIAM'S STORY

"I came out of Germany in July 1939 on one of the last Kindertransports. I am sure the Quakers had something to do with the fact that I got on. But the main reason I was able to go was because I had a guarantor [sponsor] named Miss C. Fraser Lee, who was the headmistress and founder of St. Trinnean's School for Girls in Edinburgh, Scotland. She took in six girls from Germany as boarders to her school. I was one of them. She saved my life."

TOP: *The first Kindertransport arrives in Harwich, England.*
RIGHT: *Seven-year-old Irene Kirstein left Germany on December 10, 1938 – the same date as this unnamed child. Is it her? The resemblance is striking.*

PEOPLE WHO HELPED

There were many people who helped make the Kindertransport possible – people who sprang into action when it mattered the most. Some were from Britain, and others were from Holland, Germany, or other places in Europe.

Here are just a few of the brave individuals who helped.

Bertha Bracey, a Quaker leader from England, was one of the key organizers of the Kindertransport and one of the people who persuaded the British government to allow the children into the country.

After *Kristallnacht*, Bertha and other Quakers traveled to Germany to assess the situation when it wasn't safe for British Jews to go. Bertha met with Wilfred Israel, the heir to a large Berlin department store who was helping many refugees escape. Wilfred introduced Bertha to the heads of Jewish women's organizations from across Germany. The crucial meetings between Bertha and these women led to the setup of the Kindertransport.

The Quakers were further involved in almost every aspect of the rescue mission. Quaker chaperones rode with the Kinder on the trains and helped them get safely to Britain. Other Quakers greeted the trains as they arrived. And many Quaker families and schools provided shelter for the children.

The British government honored Bertha as a Hero of the Holocaust. She was also named one of the Righteous Among the Nations in Yad Vashem, Israel's memorial to Jewish Holocaust victims. This honor is awarded to non-Jews who risked their lives in order to rescue Jews in danger during the Holocaust.

Bertha Bracey, Religious Society of Friends, Britain.

Nicholas Winton was a twenty-nine-year-old stockbroker from London who saved 669 Jewish children. He was the first to organize a rescue mission from Czechoslovakia.

Nicholas traveled to Prague, the capital, in 1938. He met with Jewish parents desperate to get their children out of the country, and he made plans to help the children leave. After organizing a network of locals to support the plan, he returned to London to raise money and find shelter for the children.

Nicholas sent a small group of children to Sweden by plane and two small groups to England by air. He also sent eight trainloads of children to England. (A ninth trainload with 250 children on board was stranded in Prague when war was declared, and travel was halted. Sadly, not one of the children on the ninth train was ever heard from again.)

Today, these rescued Kinder call themselves Winton's Children, in honor of the man who saved their lives. Later they gave him a ring engraved with the words "Save one life, save the world" – a saying from the Talmud.

Queen Elizabeth II knighted Sir Nicholas Winton in 2003. He, too, was named a Hero of the Holocaust by the British government.

TOP: *A statue at the Prague railway station commemorates Sir Nicholas Winton.*
BOTTOM: *Norbert Wollheim on the deck of a ship as he accompanies Jewish children to Denmark.*

Norbert Wollheim was a twenty-five-year-old Jewish man who helped with the Kindertransport in Berlin. After *Kristallnacht*, he was anxious to leave Germany, but he stayed to help the children get out. When interviewed years later for the documentary film *Into the Arms of Strangers*, Norbert said, "It's not enough what you do for yourself. You have to try also to do something for people who are less lucky than you are or need your help and support."

Norbert organized travel permits for the children. He kept lists of the young travelers for both the British authorities and the Nazis. He coordinated travel times and meeting places, and he made late-night phone calls to England to confirm arrangements there. He gathered the children at the train station, found chaperones to travel with them, and even acted as a chaperone on some of the transports.

In 1943, Norbert was sent to Auschwitz (a Nazi death camp) with his wife and son. Of his seventy relatives sent there, he was the only one to survive.

Geertruida (Truus) Wijsmuller-Meijer was a non-Jewish social worker from Holland whose fearless actions helped save the lives of thousands of Jewish children. She was a volunteer at and later a board member of an orphanage for refugee children in Amsterdam.

Truus traveled to Vienna, Austria, in early December 1938, to convince Adolf Eichmann (a Nazi leader later convicted of war crimes) to allow Jewish children to travel to England. During their meeting, he treated her very badly, yet she persisted. By the end of the meeting, he agreed to let the children go. Within a week, a transport of six hundred children was on its way to safety.

Truus traveled to Germany again and again to get more children out. She dealt with fierce border guards, arranged shelters for the children, and helped them onto ships at the Hook of Holland and onto planes to England.

One of her most dramatic accomplishments involved gathering up a group of Jewish children from the Amsterdam orphanage and rushing them onto the last ship to England – the SS *Bodegraven* – as Holland fell to the Nazis.

For her humanitarian work, Truus was also named Righteous Among the Nations in Yad Vashem.

Truus Wijsmuller-Meijer.

THE SS *BODEGRAVEN*

Norbert Ripp, Hans Levy, and his brother, Oscar, were three of the boys who escaped to England on May 14, 1940, on the SS *Bodegraven* – an old Dutch freighter.

Just hours before the Dutch government surrendered to the Nazis, Truus Wijsmuller-Meijer, a board member for an Amsterdam orphanage, raced to rescue as many Jewish refugee children as she could. She organized buses to transport seventy-four children from the orphanage to the port at IJmuiden, where they would board a ship to England. (These children had earlier left Germany and Austria for the safety of Holland, but now Jews were in danger in Holland, too.)

On the way to the port, the buses were stopped by soldiers at roadblocks, but Truus persuaded them to allow the children to continue on their way.

HANS LEVY'S STORY

"When we arrived, Mrs. Wijsmuller-Meijer went from ship to ship to persuade the captains to take us aboard. The captain of the *Bodegraven* agreed but explained there was very little food. Once aboard the ship, Mrs. Wijsmuller-Meijer bade us farewell. We begged her to come with us. By then, we looked upon her as a mother. We set sail May 14, 1940. We tried to make ourselves as comfortable as possible, when suddenly two enemy planes dived out of the sky with machine guns blazing. We could hear bullets hitting the ship. After a moment of silence, they came once more with all guns blazing. By then, the ship crew was on deck with their rifles, shooting at the low-flying planes. But they were no match for machines armed for combat. The planes went as quickly as they had come. The German army now knew of our presence, so we were in constant danger."

NORBERT'S STORY

"After we boarded the *Bodegraven*, we roamed the deck. It was early evening. Soon a German fighter plane – I believe there were two – approached at a very low altitude and started to machine gun us while circling the ship. We threw ourselves down, and I couldn't take my eyes off the plane and its tracer bullets. It was a total miracle that no one was hurt. Soon one or two tiny British torpedo boats shot back, and the planes left. We were placed in a ship storage area for the night, where we slept lined up in a row on the floor and covered with a sack from a long roll. Meals were rice with dried fruit, and we ate three and four together from a single tin plate."

Sailing with the children from the orphanage were about 190 other Jewish refugees. Many more had tried to escape on the ship, but time had run out before they could board.

After five days at sea and terribly stormy weather, the SS *Bodegraven* docked in Liverpool, England, on May 19, 1940. They were the last Jewish children to be rescued by the Kindertransport.

TOP: *The SS Bodegraven.*
LEFT: *Hans and Oscar Levy, safe in England.*

LIFE IN BRITAIN

The Kinder began to adjust to their lives in the safety of Britain.

Young children stayed with foster families and many grew close to them. The older children usually went to hostels or boarding schools, and some made lifelong friends with other Kinder they met there.

Although the children were no longer in danger, the adjustment wasn't easy. They felt homesick and worried about their loved ones back home. Some children only spoke a little English and had trouble understanding what people said to them. The weather was colder than they were used to, the customs were different, and the food was unfamiliar. Some Kinder were teased at school for their German accents, and – because of their names – people often confused them with Nazis.

While many children were warmly welcomed by their foster families, others, sadly, were ignored or even treated harshly. Some were put to work as maids, nannies, or workers at farms and factories. Others were pressured into converting to Christianity.

Hitler invaded Poland on September 1, 1939. In doing so, he broke an international treaty, and the leaders of Britain and France declared war. There was now even more reason for the children to be worried about their families back home.

LEFT: *Dovercourt Camp, near Harwich, was used as short-term accommodation for newly arrived Kinder. That winter, the cabins were so cold that children slept in their coats.*
OPPOSITE LEFT: *These Quaker women were foster mothers to some of the Kinder in Bristol, England.*
OPPOSITE RIGHT: *"Declaration of War" by Hans Jackson, depicting himself and other boys at Kitchener Camp (for refugees) in England. They are listening to the radio when war is declared.*

HANS LEVY'S STORY

"We found ourselves settling down in a community center used by Boy Scouts and Girl Guides in the town of Wigan. The people of that wonderful northern town were kindness itself. The Barlow family took me in their car for outings into the countryside and for walks to the local park, where I saw my first cricket match. The owner of the local cinema treated us to a matinee performance of *The Hunchback of Notre Dame*. On the way back, we called in at the nearby fish-and-chips shop, and there on the counter was a row of parcels with fish and chips for us, neatly packed in the *Wigan Daily News*."

DORA'S STORY

"I arrived on a Friday afternoon and the family put me to work right away. I couldn't speak a word of English. I never went to school."

ELLEN'S STORY

"Neither of my foster parents spoke German, and adjustment was quite difficult. Not only could we not understand each other's conversation, but the customs were quite different. For instance, in Germany, 'good' children didn't hide their hands in their laps when sitting at the table; the hands were to rest at the edge of the table. When I took pains to be on my best behavior and put my hands on the table, I got slapped because that was considered unacceptable. I attended a two-room schoolhouse. All the children knew I came from Germany and they called me *Nazi*, a word I understood all too well. None of the children wanted to make friends with me."

JOSEPH'S STORY

Joseph and his group arrived in the middle of a very cold winter. On their first night, they slept in unheated cabins. Joseph became very ill and had to be taken to the hospital.

"They gave me a hot water bottle, and by morning it was a block of ice. It was too much for me. I shut down. I have no memory of the next two and a half years."

MIRIAM'S STORY

"I always felt like an outsider, but generally I was well treated. The other students were very kind."

THE WAR YEARS

World War II lasted from 1939 to 1945 and was a long and devastating conflict that involved many countries. More than fifty-five million people lost their lives. The world had never seen such a big or deadly war.

No one had expected that the Kinder would need to stay in Britain for all those years. But during the war, travel across borders became almost impossible. The parents who had hoped to join their children in Britain were stuck in Nazi-ruled countries.

When the war began, on September 1, 1939, the British government believed that the country's major cities would be bombed by the German army, so they moved large numbers of children and pregnant women to safe areas in the countryside. Many of the Kinder were uprooted again. For a second time, they had to settle into new foster families or shelters.

The Kinder tried hard to keep in touch with their parents through letters, but this became more and more difficult as the war progressed. Soon the children could only send twenty-five-word messages through the Red Cross or via relatives in other countries. After 1942, many children stopped hearing from their parents altogether and were totally cut off from their families.

As the years passed, the Kinder became more settled in Britain. Young children became teenagers and teenagers became young adults. They spoke English, went to school or worked, and made friends. Some grew very close to their foster families.

TOP: *"Quilt 2, Square 14" by Kirsten Grosz, made in memory of her mother-in-law, who perished in Auschwitz. Kirsten's husband, Hanus, was saved by the Kindertransport.*
BOTTOM: *"Quilt 3, Square 6" by Marianne Elsley, representing a photographic image she received in a last letter from her parents before they died in Auschwitz. Marianne's father was a photographer.*

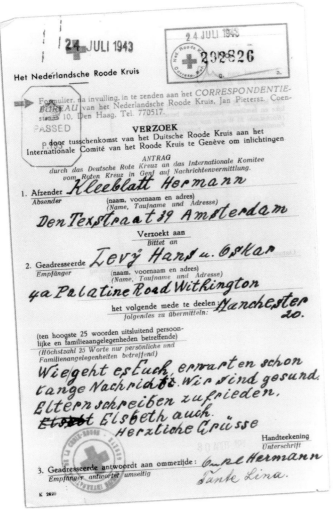

The children waited anxiously for the war to be over and for their reunion with parents and relatives. Sadly, for many of the Kinder, this reunion would never come.

When the war ended, the world was horrified to find out that millions of Jews had not survived. They had lost their lives under Nazi terror in what is now known as the Holocaust. Many of the children heard the unbearable news that one or both of their parents had died.

TOP: *Hans and Oscar Levy received this Red Cross letter in July 1943 from their aunt and uncle, who were refugees in Amsterdam. In German, it reads: "How are you? We await news from you. Your parents wrote that they are fine, as is Elsbeth." (Elsbeth survived, but sadly the boys' parents did not.)*

BOTTOM: *On September 4, 1942, just before Hedy's mother was deported to Auschwitz, she sent her daughter this letter. In German, it reads: "Traveling to the east . . . sending you a final good-bye."*

AFTER THE WAR

After the war, many of the Kinder were left to find their own way in the world. Some of the children were the only survivors of their families, having lost parents, brothers, sisters, cousins, aunts, uncles, and grandparents. For many children, there was no reunion or returning to the country of their birth.

Some parents of the Kinder survived, but it often took years to reunite with their children. Few people had money or resources for travel at the end of the war, and family members were often scattered around the world, having fled to wherever they could to find safety.

Once again, Britain stepped forward and made a generous offer. In 1946, the British government offered citizenship to any young person over fifteen years of age who had lost his or her parents, had been forced to leave his or her home, and had been living in Britain for five years. Many of the Kinder gratefully became British citizens and made Britain their permanent home. Other Kinder moved from Britain to Israel, Canada, the United States, or Australia to join relatives or family friends, or simply to make a new start.

For many years, people believed that most of the Kinder never saw their parents or other family members again. A recent survey by the Association of Jewish Refugees, however, revealed a more positive outcome. The study found that although approximately two-thirds of the Kinder did not see their parents again, one-third of the children came to Britain with a sibling and about two-thirds of the Kinder found other relatives after the war.

In honor of
FANNY & ABE
DAVIS
London. England
who saved my life
Hans Weinmann

FAR LEFT: *Joseph as a young man.*
LEFT: *"Quilt 1, Square 2" by Hans R. Weinmann, who thanks his sponsors for making it possible for him to flee Vienna to the safety of England.*

HANS LEVY'S STORY

"Manchester, England, soon became my home town, the town where I grew up, where I went to school, to cheder [school for Jewish children], to the synagogue, and where I started my first job and continued with the study of music. With the war coming to an end, my brother and I were reunited with my sister, Elsbeth, who had spent most of the war in concentration camps. She was able to confirm that our parents had met their death in that camp [Auschwitz]. One of the proudest days of my life came in May of 1947, when I swore an allegiance to His Majesty King George VI, and I became a British citizen."

JOSEPH'S STORY

Joseph learned the terrible news that his parents had not survived the war. His father had become ill and died in Camp de Gurs in Vichy, France, and his mother had been put to death in Auschwitz.

"I was seriously depressed. In those days, you didn't know about psychologists. You were on your own. I rode a bike and tried to talk myself into feeling better. I became a voracious reader and read self-help books. A free public library – it was what saved me. The other thing that kept me going was that I wanted to make a difference, to make an impact."

Joseph later joined relatives in California and went on to become a teacher and a university professor – a wonderful way to make an impact.

Ruth (right), her sister Hannah, and her brother Ernest meet after years of separation.

MIRIAM'S STORY

Miriam saw her mother and brother in Scotland after ten years of being apart. She saw her father a bit later (he had remarried). Even though her family had survived the war, they had suffered terribly during that time.

> "I would like people to think the Holocaust could never happen again. But if it did happen and you had the chance to save a life, you might think about it. It could make a difference."

RUTH'S STORY

Ruth's parents also tragically perished, but she kept all of the letters they wrote to their children – who were spread out in North and South America and in the north and south of England – during the war. (Her parents kept the two youngest children with them as long as they could, and then the children went into hiding and were saved.)

> "We never met again as a six-some, as the oldest brothers died early, but we eventually met again as a foursome. We no longer had a common language. We are a typical example of the Diaspora, the scattering of Jews around the world."

THE KINDER TODAY

More than seventy years have passed since the Kindertransport, and many of the Kinder are now grandmothers and grandfathers.

The story of the Kindertransport is a good example of the Jewish phrase "Whoever saves one life saves the world entire." The story teaches us the value of helping others who are suffering from injustice and shows us how saving those ten thousand children led to the creation of so many more lives.

As well as forming loving families, the Kinder worked and studied hard and made important contributions to society. They became teachers, doctors, dentists, lawyers, professors, journalists, scientists, musicians, authors, filmmakers, politicians, artists, and athletes. Many were also successful businesspeople, and a few of the Kinder have even won the Nobel Prize. As a group, their gifts and talents are impressive!

Today, many of the Kinder speak to groups of children or adults about their experiences in Nazi Europe and about their rescue. In their talks, they encourage the audience members to help others in need. They discuss the importance of standing up for people who are bullied or persecuted. They do not want us to forget what happened to them and to their families.

You may be wondering what happened to the Kinder you've met in this book and about their lives now.

Ellen, Joseph, Miriam, Norbert, Doris, and Hedy all live in the United States. Hans Levy, Ruth, and Hans Jackson (the artist) live in England. Irene lives in Canada. Most of them have close families with children and grandchildren they are proud of.

Ellen became a politician and a cycling activist. Joseph became a political science professor. Irene is a children's author and playwright. Miriam is an accomplished violinist, and Norbert is a retired dentist and assistant professor of dentistry. Ruth is a retired teacher of modern languages, Doris is a retired seamstress, and Hans Levy became an engraver and a manager of a shoe store. Hedy is an activist who travels the world and speaks out about injustice wherever she sees it. All of them gladly shared their stories. Here are some of their messages to you.

ELLEN FLETCHER (formerly Ellen Auster)
"I feel it's a privilege speaking to young people, so they can get a direct feeling of what was going on in Nazi Germany at that time."

HANS LEVY
"Never take your good life and freedom for granted. There are still so many countries in the world where millions of people go hungry and where freedom of speech is prohibited. Live your life by the sayings of our forefathers, who said: 'Do not do unto others as you would not do unto yourself.'"

JOSEPH HABERER
"The Kindertransport shows what can be done to rescue parentless or refugee children at risk when there is a will to do so. It was, after all, citizens, churches, and other nongovernment groups that took action and pressured the government to act quickly. In your own neighborhood, if you encounter prejudice, speak up. Don't just sit there; say something or do something. You can always do more than you think you can do."

DORIS SMALL (formerly Dora Gostynski)
"I would like to leave a message to our children and grandchildren to remember the past. To remember when the world fell into darkness a little more than seventy years ago. When brutality and hatred went out of control. *Kristallnacht*, gas chambers, and concentration camps by Nazi control. They brought death and suffering to many millions of men, women, and children – Jewish and non-Jewish alike. We must stand guard that this shall never happen again. And by learning from the past, together we must build a bright future in peace and respect for all mankind."

MIRIAM SCHNEIDER (formerly Miriam Wieck)

"You can rescue yourself in music." Miriam still plays the violin she took with her on the Kindertransport.

RUTH DAVID (formerly Ruth Oppenheimer)

"I feel we must learn to meet, understand, and appreciate people who are different from us, people who may look different, think differently, believe in a different faith, but who are what we all are: human beings with the same needs for life, love, and the freedom to live without fear. If we are fortunate and feel we already have such rights and opportunities, we should make it our task to help others less fortunate than ourselves."

HEDY EPSTEIN (formerly Hedy Wachenheimer)

"Speak up. Challenge people and governments when they do something wrong or speak ill of someone. This is very difficult to do and takes a lot of courage. I am convinced that each and every one of us not only can but must make a difference!"

IRENE N. WATTS (formerly Irene Kirstein)

"We [the Kinder] all have something in common: we are grateful for the new lives we were given." Irene has written three books for children about the Kindertransport.

NORBERT RIPP

"Cherish your family, tell them that you love them, and be the best you can be to help make this a better world."

REUNIONS

In 1989, fifty years after the Kindertransport, Bertha Leverton, one of the Kinder from Germany, organized a fiftieth anniversary reunion. About twelve hundred people (Kinder and their families from across the world) gathered in England to greet old friends and remember their Kindertransport experience.

Margaret Thatcher, the prime minister of England at the time, sent a message that was read out to the attendees. She wrote, "I am pleased and proud that the government of the time offered you refuge and help following the dreadful persecution you suffered in Germany and central Europe. You came to us as homeless children and grew up to enrich the life of this country with your courage and fortitude."

The fiftieth anniversary was so successful that a Reunion of Kindertransport (ROK) organization was formed, and other reunions followed. The Kindertransport Association (KTA) was also established in the United States, where many of the Kinder now live. The KTA has regional chapters and hosts regular reunions that include second- and third-generation members (the children and grandchildren of the Kinder).

For many years, the Kinder didn't speak much about their childhood experiences, but the reunions have helped to change that.

A very special reunion of the Czech Kindertransport took place in the summer of 2009, seventy years after the original transport. This reunion was organized to promote the theme Inspiration by Goodness and to celebrate the one-hundred-year birthday of the group's hero, Sir Nicholas Winton. Twenty-two Kinder, now senior citizens, and their families (about 170 people in all) took the commemorative trip from Prague to London, recreating the 1939 rescue that had been organized by Nicholas Winton.

The journey, by vintage steam trains and boat, took four days. The passengers traveled by train through Germany and the Netherlands, and then rode a ship to England.

The Winton Train.

TOP: *Eleven-year-old passenger Sophie Grosz-Dequenne (far left) is shown here with Sir Nicholas Winton (seated) and other family members and friends. Sophie's grandfather, Hanus Grosz, was rescued by Winton.*

BOTTOM: *Hans Levy (left) and Norbert Ripp (center) recently had a reunion with Werner Katz (now Stephen Kates), who they had not seen since they traveled together on the SS Bodegraven more than seventy years ago.*

But unlike the young Kinder on the original journey, who had carried their own food and slept on hard, wooden train benches, these passengers ate three-course meals served in the dining car and slept in hotels at night.

At the Hook of Holland, the travelers boarded an overnight ferry that arrived in Harwich, England, at 6 a.m. on September 4, 2009. From there, they rode The Winton Train (a tribute train made up of vintage passenger cars and a brand-new steam engine) to Liverpool Street station – the place where the Kinder had arrived so long ago.

Waiting for the travelers at the station was Sir Nicholas Winton himself – now one hundred years old!

"It's wonderful to see you all after seventy years," he said as the travelers stepped off the train.

It was an emotional meeting for the Kinder and the man who had rescued them. There were tears of gratitude, flowers, and heartfelt thanks from the Kinder, who said such things as "He gave us life" and "He is like a father to me."

REMEMBERING

The rescue of ten thousand children on the Kindertransport was possible because good and caring people took steps to help in desperate times.

The Kinder, now in their senior years, want us to know that there is always something we can do to help others who suffer from persecution or unfair treatment. They have shared their stories to show us that great things can be accomplished if there is a will to do it.

On June 14, 1991, members of the KTA and ROK created a plaque to honor Britain. It hangs in the Palace of Westminster (Houses of Parliament) in London.

There is also a Kindertransport sculpture at Liverpool Street station in London. It was created by Frank Meisler, who was rescued as a child from the Free City of Danzig on the Kindertransport. It shows five children with their suitcases and musical instruments, standing on a piece of train track. Surrounding them are sixteen blocks, each one naming a Kindertransport departure city. The statue is a poignant reminder of the children who arrived at this train station without their parents so many years ago.

TOP: *Memorial plaque that honors Britain for saving the Kinder.*
BOTTOM: *"Children of the Kindertransport" created by Frank Meisler.*

In deep gratitude
to the people and Parliament
of the United Kingdom
for saving the lives of
10,000 Jewish and other children
who fled to this country
from Nazi persecution
on the Kindertransport
1938–1939

LEFT: *One of the five Kindertransport Memory Quilts.*
TOP: *Sophie Grosz-Dequenne.*

The five Kindertransport memory quilts, sewn by Kirsten Grosz, piece together unique and beautiful squares made by some of the Kinder and their family members. The quilts are on display at the Holocaust Memorial Center in Farmington Hills, Michigan. An audio clip or a written explanation accompanies each square, telling the story of the square's creator. You can see the quilts (and hear or read the stories) at www.holocaustcenter.org or in the book *Kindertransport Memory Quilt* by Hanus, Kirsten, and Anita Grosz.

Sophie Grosz-Dequenne, granddaughter of the quilt-maker, is alive because her grandfather, Hanus Grosz, was rescued by the Kindertransport. There are thousands of children like Sophie who owe their lives to the rescue.

After riding on the Winton Reunion Train, Sophie said, "Thinking about my grandfather and the other children waving good-bye to their parents in Prague was sad. Still, you always learn from experiences that you don't like. Don't give up hope. It was remarkable what Nicholas Winton did."

The gift of Sophie's life, and the lives of so many other children and grandchildren, is a wonderful legacy of the Kinder who were saved and the people who saved them.

The tributes created by the Kinder provide a lasting record of the kindness of strangers and a memorial to the beloved parents and families who were lost to the Kinder so long ago. They help us remember the past and they encourage us to strive for a world full of compassion and caring – and acceptance for all.

Whoever saves one life saves the world entire.

WORDS TO KNOW

anti-Semitism: hatred of Jews as a group, often expressed in discrimination or hateful actions against Jews

Aryan: a word adopted by the Nazis to describe any person who was an ethnic blue-eyed, blond-haired German; those who did not fit this description were considered non-Aryan, or inferior

Auschwitz: the largest Nazi concentration and extermination (death) camp, located in Poland, where almost one million Jews were murdered by the Nazis

boycott: to avoid or protest against a certain person, business, or organization

concentration camp: a Nazi prison camp where innocent people lost their lives due to starvation, overwork, or murder

Evian Conference: a meeting in France in 1938, where representatives from thirty-two countries discussed the situation of Jewish refugees but did little to help

Great Depression: a time of widespread unemployment and poverty, from 1929 to 1939, caused by a steep drop in the world economy

Hitler, Adolf: the German dictator who, with his collaborators, was responsible for the death of six million Jews

Hitler Youth: the Nazi Party's youth organization

Holocaust: the state-sponsored persecution and murder of six million Jews by the Nazi regime and their collaborators, from 1933 to 1945

humanitarian: a person who takes action to help others and make the world a better place

Kinder: the children

Kindertransport: the organized rescue of ten thousand Jewish children from Germany, Austria, Czechoslovakia, and the Free City of Danzig (now Gdańsk, Poland) before World War II

Kristallnacht: November 9 to 10, 1938, also known as the Night of Broken Glass, the night of Nazi-led riots and attacks on Jews; another name for this night is *Reichspogromnacht*

Nazi Party: Hitler's political party in Germany from 1919 to 1945, which rose to power in 1933 and held extreme views, especially hatred of Jews and other minorities (the party's actual name was National Socialist German Workers' Party)

persecution: the cruel treatment of a person or group of people because of their religious beliefs or race or for other reasons

Quakers: a faith group, also known as the Religious Society of Friends, whose members believe in working for peace, justice, and equality in the world

refugee: a person who flees danger or persecution in a country to find safety in another country

SA: the Nazi Party paramilitary, also known as "Storm Troopers" and "Brownshirts," who helped Hitler rise to power in Germany

sponsor: a person or organization that pledges money and support to help someone else

synagogue: a Jewish place of worship

treaty: a formal agreement between nations that refers to peace, trade, or other international business

visa: an official document allowing a citizen of one country to enter another country

World War II: the biggest, deadliest war in history, from 1939 to 1945, with fighting in many countries and more than fifty-five million deaths

Yad Vashem: Israel's official memorial to the Jewish victims of the Holocaust, including a museum, synagogue, and memorial sites

"Mob Gathering at Kristallnacht" by Hans Jackson.

MAP OF THE ROUTE OF THE KINDERTRANSPORT

EUROPE AND GREAT BRITAIN IN 1933

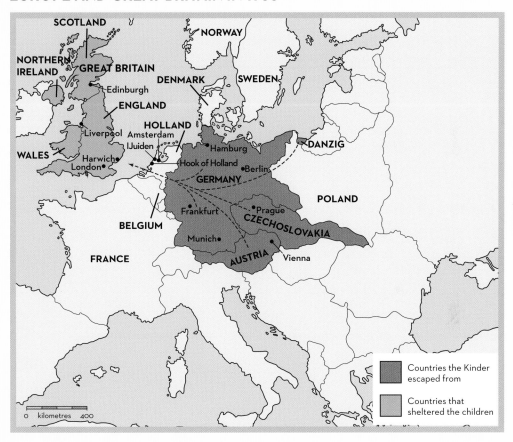

Children on the Kindertransport escaped from Germany, Austria, Czechoslovakia, and the Free City of Danzig (now Gdańsk, Poland). Most of them traveled by train through Germany and Holland, then boarded a ship at the Hook of Holland. The ship crossed the ocean and docked at Harwich, England. From there, many of the Kinder rode a train to London. Although it is not well-known or documented at this time, there may have been additional transports of children to the Netherlands, France, Belgium, Sweden, and Denmark. Researchers, such as Miriam Keesing in the Netherlands, are working to establish this.

TIMELINE

Here are just a few of the many anti-Jewish events and laws put in place by Hitler and the Nazis in the 1930s.

1933
- Hitler becomes chancellor (leader) of Germany
- Violence against Jews by the SA begins
- Books written by Jews and anti-Nazi writers are burned
- Jewish students and professors are forced out of universities
- Jews are forced out of jobs in the civil service
- Jews are banned from the fields of journalism, art, music, literature, broadcasting, and theater
- Boycott of Jewish shops and businesses begins
- Boycott of Jewish doctors and lawyers begins
- First concentration camp opens (by 1945, there are more than a thousand camps)

1934
- Jews are banned from having health insurance
- Jewish holidays are removed from the German calendar

1935
- The Nuremberg Laws are passed, taking away the right of Jewish people to be German citizens and forbidding Jews to marry non-Jews
- Jews can no longer vote or hold public office

1936
- Nazis remove public anti-Jewish signs during the Berlin Olympics, to keep the world from knowing what they are doing

1937
- Jews are banned from working in any office
- Nazis begin taking away properties and businesses from Jews

1938

- Germany takes control of Austria; Jews in Austria are now persecuted
- Jews are forced to carry identity cards at all times
- Jewish passports must be stamped with a red letter *J*
- Jewish women must add *Sara* to their names; Jewish men must add *Israel*
- Jewish children are expelled from German public schools
- Jews are banned from public places (theaters, parks, pools, and so on)
- Jews are forced to close and sell their businesses
- *Kristallnacht*, November 9 to 10, 1938: a night of extreme violence against Jews in Germany, Austria, and the Sudetenland; Jews are forced to clean up and pay for the damage

1938 to 1939

- Kindertransport, December 1, 1938, to September 1, 1939: ten thousand Jewish children are rescued from Germany, Austria, Czechoslovakia, and the Free City of Danzig (now Gdańsk, Poland) and sent to safety in Britain

1939

- Germany invades Czechoslovakia
- Germany invades Poland
- Jews in Czechoslovakia and Poland are now persecuted
- Britain and France declare war on Germany

1939 to 1945

- World War II begins on September 1, 1939; Germany invades many countries of Europe and persecutes the Jews living there
- Beginning in 1941, all Jews must wear a yellow Star of David

1945

- Germany surrenders on May 7, 1945; the war in Europe is over
- The world discovers that six million Jews have lost their lives at the hands of the Nazis in what is now known as the Holocaust

1945 to 1946

- Nuremberg Trials: Nazi leaders are put on trial and punished for their crimes against humanity

NOTE TO PARENTS AND TEACHERS

Of the six million Jews put to death by Hitler's Nazis, one and a half million were children. The rescue of ten thousand children on the Kindertransport shines a ray of light on this darkest of times. It gives us hope for a brighter future.

There is no easy way to tell a young person about the Holocaust. It is a topic that requires the discretion of parents and teachers who will know the best time and approach for discussing this sensitive subject.

To find out more about the Kindertransport and the author's sources, please see the following listings.

Books for Children

Finding Sophie by Irene N. Watts

Good-bye Marianne by Irene N. Watts (also in graphic novel format, illustrated by Kathryn E. Shoemaker)

The Last Goodbye: The Rescue of Children from Nazi Europe by the Jewish Museum, London

One Small Suitcase by Barry Turner

Remember Me by Irene N. Watts

Ten Thousand Children: True Stories Told by Children Who Escaped the Holocaust on the Kindertransport by Anne L. Fox and Eva Abraham-Podietz

Books for Adults

And the Policeman Smiled by Barry Turner

The Routledge Atlas of the Holocaust by Martin Gilbert

Child of Our Time: A Young Girl's Flight from the Holocaust by Ruth David

Encyclopedia of the Holocaust by Robert Rozett and Shmuel Spector

Into the Arms of Strangers: Stories of the Kindertransport by Mark Jonathan Harris and Deborah Oppenheimer, based on the feature-length documentary film by Warner Bros. Pictures

Kindertransport Memory Quilt by Hanus, Kirsten, and Anita Grosz

Kristallnacht: Prelude to Destruction by Martin Gilbert

Nicholas Winton and the Rescued Generation by Muriel Emanuel and Vera Gissing

"Quilt 1, Square 1" by Kirsten Grosz, on display at the Holocaust Memorial Center.

DVDs for Adults

Into the Arms of Strangers: Stories of the Kindertransport, Warner Bros. Pictures

My Knees Were Jumping: Remembering the Kindertransports, IFC Films

The Power of Good: Nicholas Winton, National Center for Jewish Film

Web Sites

Association of Jewish Refugees (Kindertransport Survey): www.ajr.org.uk

German and Austrian War Children in the Netherlands (research by Miriam Keesing): http://dokin.nl

Hans Jackson: http://hansjacksongallery.multiply.com/photos

Holocaust Memorial Center (Kindertransport Memorial Quilts): www.holocaustcenter.org

Imperial War Museum: www.iwm.org.uk

Kindertransport Association: www.kindertransport.org

United States Holocaust Memorial Museum: www.ushmm.org

Wiener Library: www.wienerlibrary.co.uk

ACKNOWLEDGMENTS

I would like to express my deep gratitude and appreciation to the following people for their help in creating this book.

Thank you to:

Dr. Joseph Haberer, Professor Emeritus of Political Science, Purdue University, Director of the Jewish Studies Program, and editor of *Shofar: An Interdisciplinary Journal of Jewish Studies,* for his review of my manuscript, for his inspired guidance on the purpose of telling this story, and for introducing me to the Kinder whose words bring this work to life.

The Kinder who so generously shared their stories and without whom this book would not be possible: Ruth David, Hedy Epstein, Ellen Fletcher, Joseph Haberer, Hans Levy, Norbert Ripp, Miriam Schneider, and Doris Small.

The talented people who allowed their artwork to grace these pages: Hans Jackson (artist) and his nephew, Allen Sternstein, who was the liason for Hans's art; all the quilt square creators; and Anita and Kirsten Grosz for giving permission to use the quilt images and for putting me in touch with the creators.

Marek Jaros, photo archivist at the Wiener Library in London, for his help with the images; Paul Kent, who provided information on the SS *Bodegraven*; Miriam Keesing, for reviewing the passage on Truus Wijsmuller-Meijer; Katherine and Ian Garner, for shepherding me around London museums; Sophie Grosz-Dequenne, for sharing her insights on the Winton Reunion train ride; and all the contributors who graciously previewed and commented on their sections of the book.

Editors Kelly Jones, Kathryn Cole, and Tara Walker for their encouragement and expertise.

Irene N. Watts, with special thanks, for being the inspiration for this book and for providing support, wise counsel, an eloquent foreword, and many primary research materials.

And, finally, to my family, for their understanding and love.

Thank you, all!

"Into the Arms of Strangers" by Hans Jackson.

PHOTOGRAPHY AND ART CREDITS

[i] Two Jewish refugee girls hugging on the boat (#WL77) © The Wiener Library; 2 Irene Kirstein at school, courtesy of Irene N. Watts; 4 Jewish refugee children in Holland on their way to England, December 1938 (#WL56) © The Wiener Library; 4 "Quilt 1, Square 15" by Ilse F. Camis (Gross) © Ilse F. Camis (Gross); 5 Beate Siegel (right) and two other girls look out a train window as they leave Germany on a Kindertransport to England (#26390) © United States Holocaust Memorial Museum, courtesy of Bea Siegel Green; 6 Ruth Oppenheimer, courtesy of Ruth David; 6 Ellen Auster, courtesy of Ellen Fletcher; 6 Joseph Haberer, courtesy of Joseph Haberer; 6 Hedy Wachenheimer, courtesy of Hedy Epstein; 7 Miriam Wieck, courtesy of Miriam Schneider; 7 Hans Levy, courtesy of Hans Levy; 7 Norbert Ripp, courtesy of Norbert Ripp; 7 Dora Gostynski, courtesy of Doris Small; 8 "Burning of the Books" by Hans Jackson © Hans Jackson; 9 "Boycott" by Hans Jackson © Hans Jackson; 9 "Leaving Germany for Kitchener Camp" by Hans Jackson © Hans Jackson; 10 "School Expulsion" by Hans Jackson © Hans Jackson; 11 "Harassing the Children" by Hans Jackson © Hans Jackson; 12 Jewish refugee girls arriving at customs in Great Britain during the Kindertransports (#WL33) © The Wiener Library; 13 Ellen Auster's mother's passport, courtesy of Ellen Fletcher; 15 "Burning Synagogue Kristallnacht" by Hans Jackson © Hans Jackson; 15 "Parent's Home and Shop Kristallnacht" by Hans Jackson © Hans Jackson; 16 Youngest refugee children during the Kindertransport in 1938 (#WL1582) © The Wiener Library; 17 Two hundred Jewish refugee children, who are members of the first Kindertransport from Germany, arrive in Harwich, England (#51114) © United States Holocaust Memorial Museum, courtesy of Instytut Pamieci Narodowej; 19 Jewish refugee youngsters on a train from Germany/Austria during the Kindertransports (#WL32) © The Wiener Library; 19 "Quilt 1, Square 8" by Margaret and Kenneth Lowe © by Margaret and Kenneth Lowe; 20 Jewish refugee child from Germany, now in Great Britain, 2 December 1938 (#WL44) © The Wiener Library; 21 Irene, her brother, and their mother reading a book, courtesy of Irene N. Watts; 21 "Quilt 1, Square 6" by Ruth Adler © Ruth Adler; 22 Heinz Stephan Lewy poses with his father and stepmother in their home in Berlin, shortly before his departure on a Kindertransport to France (#24808) © United States Holocaust Memorial Museum, courtesy of Stephan H. Lewy; 22 Circular label removed from the suitcase used by Margot Stern when she was sent on a Kindertransport to England (#N02805) © United States Holocaust Memorial Museum, courtesy of Margot Stern Loewenberg; 23 "Children Leaving Anhalter Bahnhof" by Hans Jackson © Hans Jackson; 24 Jewish refugee children taking leave from their parents, Schlesischer Bahnhof, Berlin November 1938 (#WL52) © The Wiener Library; 25 "Quilt 2, Square 16" by Helga Newman © Helga Newman; 26 Jewish refugee boy playing the violin amongst other boys on train out of Germany (#WL31) © The Wiener Library; 26 Jewish refugee children falling asleep on the train taking them out of Germany in December 1938 (#WL65) © The Wiener Library; 26 Jewish refugee children on transit are welcomed in Rotterdam, 2 December 1938 (#WL63) © The Wiener Library; 29 "Quilt 1, Square 3" by Berta S. Wesler and Karen Wesler © Berta S. Wesler and Karen Wesler; 30 Members of the first Kindertransport arrive in Harwich, England (#06210) © United States Holocaust Memorial Museum, courtesy of Frances Rose; 30 A sleeping refugee girl during the Kindertransport in November/December 1938 (#WL66) © The Wiener Library; 31 Bertha Bracey © Religious Society of Friends in Britain; 32 Nicholas Winton statue, photograph © Luděk Kovář; 32 Norbert Wollheim sits on deck of a ship while accompanying German-Jewish children to a summer camp Kinderlager [children's recreational summer camp] in Horserod, Denmark (#66412) © United States Holocaust Memorial Museum, courtesy of Norbert Wollheim; 33 Truus Wijsmuller-Meijer, photograph by Miriam Keesing, courtesy of the collection of the NIOD in Amsterdam; 35 Hans and Oscar Levy, courtesy of Hans Levy; 35 The SS *Bodegraven*, courtesy of Miriam Keesing, from the collection of W.H. Moojen, Beverwijk; 36 Jewish refugee children from Germany at Dovercourt Bay, near Harwich, shortly after arrival in Great Britain in December 1938 (#WL927) © The Wiener Library; 37 Two British Quaker women who served as foster parents to Jewish Kindertransport children, pose with a group of young children in Bristol (#09403) © United States Holocaust Memorial Museum, courtesy of Peter Kollisch; 37 "Declaration of War" by Hans Jackson © Hans Jackson; 39 "Quilt 2, Square 14" by Kirsten Grosz © Kirsten Grosz; 39 "Quilt 3, Square 6" by Marianne Elsley © Marianne Elsley; 40 Red Cross letter sent by a German Jewish refugee couple in Amsterdam to their grandnephews in Manchester, England (#38541) © United States Holocaust Memorial Museum, courtesy of Hans Levy; 40 Hedy's mother's final letter, photograph courtesy of Hedy Epstein; 41 Joseph Haberer, courtesy of Joseph Haberer; 41 "Quilt 1, Square 2" by Hans R. Weinmann © Hans R. Weinmann; 43 Ruth with sister and brother, courtesy of Ruth David; 45 Ellen Fletcher © Richard Masoner; 45 Hans Levy, courtesy of Hans Levy; 45 Joseph Haberer © Carroll County Comet, Delphi, IN; 45 Doris Small, courtesy of Doris Small; 46 Miriam Schneider, courtesy of Miriam Schneider; 46 Ruth David, courtesy of Ruth David; 46 Hedy Epstein, courtesy of Hedy Epstein; 46 Irene N. Watts © Russell J.C. Kelly; 46 Norbert Ripp, courtesy of Norbert Ripp; 47 Winton Train, photograph in the public domain; 48 Sophie Grosz-Dequenne with Sir Nicholas Winton, courtesy of Anita Grosz; 48 Hans Levy, Norbert Ripp, and Stephen Kates © Batya Warshowsky; 49 Plaque image recreated with permission from the Association of Jewish Refugees; 49 Frank Meisler sculpture, photograph © Frank Meisler; 50 "Kindertransport Memory Quilt #1" © Anita and Kirsten Grosz; 50 Sophie Grosz-Dequenne, courtesy of Anita Grosz; 52 "Mob Gathering on Kristallnacht" by Hans Jackson © Hans Jackson; 57 "Quilt 1, Square 1" by Kirsten Grosz © Kirsten Grosz; 58 "Into the Arms of Strangers" by Hans Jackson © Hans Jackson.

NOTE:
To see more of Hans Jackson's art, visit **http://hansjacksongallery.multiply.com/photos**.
To see more of the Kindertransport Memory Quilts, visit **www.holocaustcenter.org/kinderTransport/index.html**.

INDEX